JACOB
and ESAU

illustrated by Leon Baxter

adapted by Diana Craig

Silver Burdett Company

Long ago, there lived a man called Isaac and his wife Rebekah. They were very happy together, except for one thing – they had no children. They almost gave up hope of ever having a family, but each day Isaac prayed that God would help them. At last he had an answer to his prayers, for Rebekah gave birth to twin boys.

The first twin to be born was not a pretty sight. In fact, he was rather ugly. He was covered with red hair – not just on his head, but all over his body as well. When Rebekah tried to cuddle him, he kicked and screamed. She decided to call him Esau, which means "hairy".

The second baby was born minutes after the arrival of the first baby. He was so unlike his brother, it was hard to believe they were twins. He had a beautiful face, with big, shiny eyes, and his skin was as smooth as silk. He lay peacefully in his mother's arms, smiling contentedly, as good as gold.

Rebekah loved him at the very first sight. She decided to call him Jacob.

As the boys grew up, they seemed even less like twins than ever. Esau was rough and wild, running and jumping all over the place; his mother soon gave up trying to stop him from clambering up the rocks. One day, Isaac took the boy out hunting. From then on, Esau spent all his time in the mountains, stalking wild animals. Whatever he killed on his trips, he brought home to make into a tasty stew for Isaac. Then the two of them would sit by the fire for hours, boasting of hunting adventures.

Jacob was quiet and gentle, and spent his time tending the sheep and the goats. Sometimes he picked herbs for his mother's cooking, or collected water for her from the well.

But Esau thought his brother was a coward, and he was always showing off and picking fights with him. "There's baby Jacob, hiding behind the sheep!" he'd sneer, as he strode off with his arrows across his back. When he got back, he'd boast "I killed a lion today . . . what did *you* do?"

Isaac was so proud of Esau. "He is my first son, so I will leave everything to him when I die," he thought. But Rebekah knew what Isaac planned. "It's not fair," she thought, "what about Jacob? What about leaving him something, instead of giving it all to that Esau!"

One evening, as Jacob sat outside the tent stirring a lentil stew, Esau painfully limped home. He had tracked a wild deer all day and, for once, the animal had escaped. To make things worse, Esau had cut his foot on a stone. He was exhausted, and the smell of Jacob's stew wafted over and reminded him that he was starving, too.

"Give me some of that, you," he barked, "or I'll pour it all over your curly hair!"

It was the last straw. Jacob had had enough of Esau. This time he wasn't going to let him get away with his bullying.

"All right, you can have some," Jacob snapped, "but only if you make me a promise first. Promise that when Father dies, you will give all his belongings to me!"

"Yes, yes, I promise, I promise. Take them all!" snapped Esau, too faint with hunger and pain to think straight. "What good will they do me if I starve to death first?"

Esau gobbled up his stew and went straight to bed. It was only when he woke in the morning that Esau realized what he had given away, just for a bowlful of stew.

The years passed, and Isaac grew very old. His eyes became so weak that in the end he could hardly see at all.

One day, he called Esau to his side. "My son, before I die there is something important I must do," he said. "I must give you my blessing so that when I am gone you can take my place as head of the family. Go hunting now, and make me one of your delicious stews. Then I will eat it and bless you."

Esau ran off at once to do as his father told him. But he didn't know that Rebekah had been listening, and had heard every word Isaac had said.

Rebekah knew this was her last chance to do something for Jacob, so she rushed to find him and explain her plan.

"Do exactly as I say," she said. "Take the stew I am about to make and give it to your father. His eyes are so bad, he won't know who you really are. You can pretend you are Esau, and you will get his blessing instead."

Jacob couldn't believe what his mother was telling him to do. He'd never get away with such a trick.

"What if Father touches me?" he protested. "My skin is much smoother than Esau's!"

"Let me worry about that," Rebekah answered. "Now get a move on. We've no time to lose."

As usual, Jacob did as his mother told him. Rebekah dressed him in Esau's best clothes, and tied hairy goatskins around his hands and neck so his skin would feel as rough as his brother's. Then, carrying the bowl of stew, Jacob crept into Isaac's tent.

"Who is that?" asked Isaac, peering into the darkness with his dim old eyes.

"Why, your son Esau, of course," Jacob lied. "I've brought your stew. Now eat up, and then you can bless me."

But Isaac was suspicious. If this really was Esau, why was he back so soon? And the voice didn't sound right, either – it sounded more like Jacob's.

"Let me touch you," Isaac said, and Jacob came closer.

"Hmm . . ." thought Isaac, as he felt the smelly goatskins on Jacob's hands and neck, "he *sounds* like Jacob, but he *feels* like Esau . . . and, pooh, he certainly *smells* like Esau, too! Yes, it must be Esau." And he kissed Jacob and gave him his blessing.

No sooner had Jacob left, than Esau brushed aside the flap into his father's tent. When Isaac heard his gruff voice and felt the touch of his rough hand, he shook with fright. He knew he had made a terrible mistake.

"I have blessed the wrong man!" he cried in anguish. "But if you are the real Esau, who was that . . .?" And then, in a flash, they both guessed the truth.

"Oh, no!" wailed Esau. "That lying, cheating Jacob has tricked me again. Bless me too, Father, bless me too!"

"I cannot, my son," said Isaac sadly. "I've given your blessing to your brother, and nothing can take it back."

Esau went white with rage. He vowed that he would kill Jacob for what he had done.

Luckily for Jacob, Rebekah discovered what Esau was planning. Jacob would have to run away and hide, at least until Esau's anger had died down. So she went to see Isaac.

"It's about time Jacob found a wife," she said. "Let's send him to visit his uncle Laban. There are plenty of girls there to choose from."

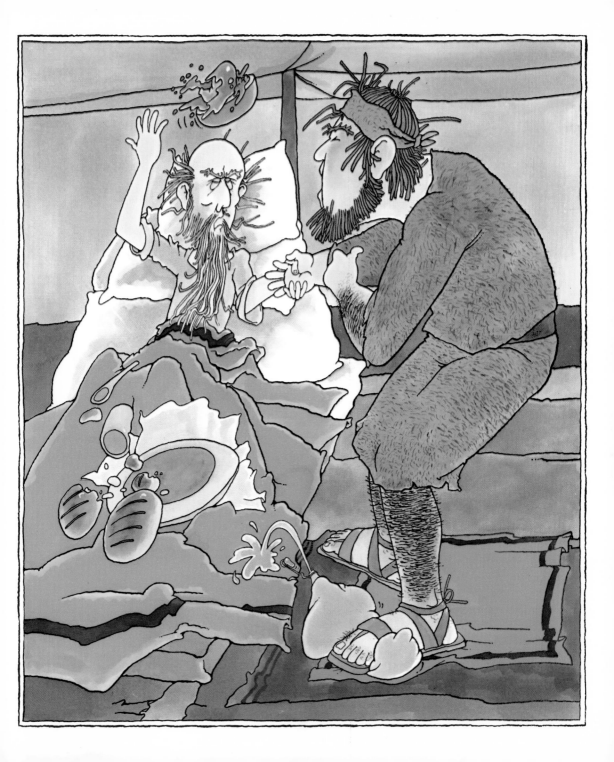

Isaac was too miserable to argue, and Jacob set off the very next day. His journey lay across a dry, rocky desert, with no trees for shade. All he carried was a water flask and a sheepskin cloak to keep him warm at night. It was lonely out in the desert with no one to talk to, and when darkness fell, Jacob could hear the wild animals howling.

Now that he had had time to think, Jacob began to feel sorry for what he had done. Esau was a bully and deserved to be taught a lesson, but perhaps he had gone too far in tricking him a second time. And now Esau was after his blood! Jacob wondered if it would ever be safe to go home again.

One night, as he lay sleeping with his head on a stone, Jacob had an amazing dream. He saw a shining staircase, stretching all the way to the stars, with angels walking up and down it. And then he heard God's voice.

"Don't be afraid," God said. "I will look after you, and I promise that one day I will bring you safely home."

When Jacob woke, he realized, with shock, that what he had seen in his dream was the entrance to heaven.

Jacob continued across the desert and finally reached his uncle's home. He was warmly welcomed, and was happy to stay and work for his uncle. In return, his uncle gave him some sheep and goats. Jacob was a good shepherd and his flocks grew so that, in a while, they were almost as big as his uncle's. He had his own servants, too, and felt quite rich. He was married now, with a large family, and had settled quite well into his new life.

Then, one day, God spoke to him again. "Come on, Jacob, it's time to pack. You are going home."

God said nothing about Esau, and Jacob felt very nervous. What if Esau was still angry? Jacob hoped God knew what he was doing, and that he hadn't forgotten his promise.

When Jacob and his family were halfway home, he heard that Esau was coming to meet them with four hundred men. Jacob was terrified, and got down on his knees and prayed.

"Please, God, I know I don't deserve it, but please, don't let me down now," he begged. "Don't let Esau kill us all."

And then, just in case God needed a little help persuading Esau to be friendly, Jacob sent his brother a present – a flock of goats, a flock of sheep, a herd of cattle, and a whole lot of camels and donkeys as well.

The next morning, Jacob lined everyone up behind him, and then bravely walked on to face his brother and his men.

At first, all he could see were small figures in the distance – an awful lot of them! Jacob shivered as he got closer and saw the men's heavy clubs and knives. Now he could pick out faces in the crowd. And then he found what he had been looking for; the red hair and the bristling beard.

Humbly, Jacob bowed to the ground, waiting to see what would happen. But instead of giving the order to attack, the big hairy man ran up and tearfully hugged his brother.

"Jacob, Jacob, it's so good to see you again after so long," cried Esau in delight. "But what were all those animals for? I was nearly trampled to death in the stampede!"

"I, I . . ." Jacob could hardly speak, he just didn't believe his brother was pleased to see him again. "I was scared. I wanted you to forgive me for that trick I played on you."

"Keep your animals, Jacob!" boomed Esau, "I've got plenty. As for your silly trick, why, we were just children then!" And he joyfully slapped his brother on the back.

Jacob still wasn't sure. "You don't understand, Esau. I was so afraid to meet you. Now I see you've been good to me, and God's been good to me, so you must let me be good to you."

And with that, Esau gratefully accepted his brother's gift.

This story has been told in many different ways for nearly three thousand years. It was first written down in a language called Hebrew. Since then, it has been retold in almost every language used in the world today.

   You can find the story of Jacob and Esau in the Bible. It is in the Book of Genesis, Chapters 25 to 33.

Editor: John Morton
Publishing Manager: Belinda Hollyer
Production: Susan Mead
Teacher Consultant: Pauline Morton
Old Testament Consultant: The Rev'd. A.K. Jenkins

A MACDONALD BOOK

© Macdonald & Co (Publishers) Ltd 1984

First published in Great Britain in 1984
by Macdonald & Co (Publishers) Ltd
London & Sydney

A BPCC plc company

Adapted and published
in the United States by
Silver Burdett Company
Morristown, N.J.

1984 Printing

ISBN 0 382 06795 9

Library of Congress
Catalog Card Number 84-51684

1 2 3 4 5 6 7 8 9 10—JDL—90 89 88 87 86 85 84